THE LITTLE
THAT IS ALL

THE LITTLE
THAT IS ALL

JOHN CIARDI

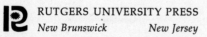
RUTGERS UNIVERSITY PRESS
New Brunswick   *New Jersey*

Second Printing

Library of Congress Cataloging in Publication Data

Ciardi, John, 1916–
   The little that is all.

   Poems.
   I. Title.
PS3505.I27L47   811'.5'2   74-6238
ISBN 0-8135-0776-6

Manufactured in the United States of America by Quinn & Boden Company, Inc.,
   Rahway, New Jersey

To
Concetta DeBenedictis Ciardi
in loving memory

ACKNOWLEDGMENTS

Some of these poems have appeared in *Antaeus, Chicago Herald Tribune, Denver Quarterly, New Orleans Quarterly, The New Yorker, Saturday Review, Saturday Review/World*

CONTENTS

WHAT WORLD IT IS

THE LITTLE
THAT IS ALL

WHAT WORLD IT IS

Or think how vultures out of nature's mind
  Descend like rancid angels to their chicks
Bearing the carrion mercy on the wind
  From stinking bones to shelves of stinking sticks.

ADDIO

The corpse my mother made
panted all one afternoon
till her father called down, "Oh, stop that!"

I saw her hear and obey
and almost smile
to lie down good again.

Then that blinked gone.
She gaped, her face
a run wax she ran from.

I kissed her forehead and thought,
"It will never be warm again."
Oh, daughter, if *I* could call!

MINUS ONE

Of seven sparrows on a country wire
        and off in the instant ruffle
of hawk shadow, one was no flyer,
        or not enough, or was lost in the shuffle,
six stunted their little panics one spin
        around a pasture and an oak, and spun
back to whatever they had been
        in much the same row minus one.

            Is there a kismet
        the size of one of seven
            sparrows? Is it
        written before heaven,
            swami, in the mystic
                billion ungiven
        Names? Is there a loving statistic
                we are motes of?
        Whatever remembers us, finally, is enough.
        If anything remembers, something is love.

Meanwhile a shadow comes to a point,
        to beak and talons. Seven surprises
start and one stops. Six joint
        excursions circle a crisis
they return forgetting. And what am I
        remembering? It was not on me
the shadow dove. I can sit by
        noting statistically.

            Is there an average
        the size of one? of any?
            Is there no rage
        against numbers? Of many

        motes, mathematician,
            shall none be
more than decided? for once its own decision?
        I have spun loose
again and again with your sparrows, father, and whose
hawk is this now? unchosen? come to choose?

A MAN CAME TUESDAY

A man came Tuesday.
Wanted what I didn't owe yet.
"By Friday you will. Pay now
and I'll discount 10%." That
made sense . . . would have . . .
except. . . . "Anything off
for good intentions?" I asked.
"I," he said, "am not
the Parole Board. I'm your
nonnegotiable future
come to a take it or leave it."
"If I had the price of a choice."
"Exactly." "But if I had,
I'd have a different future."
"That," he said, "is what I'm trying
to get you to." "Who the devil
are you?" He shrugged:
"I have no contract with the truth
but I like to be persuasive—
what are you prepared to believe?"

REMEMBERING CURZIO MALAPARTE OR
SOMETHING ELSE AT A HOWARD JOHNSON'S
COUNTER ON HOLLYWOOD BEACH

He reported as fact, the liar, a conversation
with a man nailed to a tree in a forest
of Jesus trees. He was interpreting idioms
of a German occupation. I have forgotten
the exact words and assume the dead have.
I remember there is a saint of liars
and pray to what I can. This is the world

in which the nailed man turned in a daydream
this noon at the Howard Johnson's on Hollywood Beach
and said, "Goddamn the living what they do!"
I offered my plate and to make up a dialogue.
He said, "I am a Jew. The one diet left me
is God and bitterness." I offered a hammer
to claw him free. He sneered. "Freer than what?"

I explained I was not Malaparte but only a reader,
pitched into reverie over coffee, dendrites,
and the Ho-Jo Special Double Burger Plate.
"Why insist on a plausibly reasoned convention
between us and what we do?" I pleaded.
"To live is to be happened to—and at.
Why shouldn't you let a hammer into this daydream,

come down, go home, and perhaps have children
to worry your way through a more average script?"
"—With Malaparte playing God the author?"
"Now is years later," I said. "He died in China.
Or it was somewhere else in no difference.
I could edit the script to suit you." "Idiot," he said,
and chose to die of choices that had been made for him

because Malaparte had been chosen to lie,
because I had been chosen to remember,
because the girl with the name tag on her breast
had been named Clairella (really?)
and offered all I could order from her one menu,
because our saints, if any, are where we find them,
because I need all I can lie to Heaven.

A CONVERSATION WITH LEONARDO

It was a stew of a night. The power failed,
killing the air conditioner. And the windows sealed.
I flailed off the one sheet and lay spread-eagled.

The instant I wilted to sleep Leonardo pounced,
drew his circle round me on the sheet,
tried fitting hands, feet, head to one turned ratio.

Ah, the greatness of lost causes! "I could have told you,"
I said, "if what you're after is ideal proportion,
you're sketching the wrong times." He frowned.

"A collector," he said, "can always use deformity
among examples, but only if lost within it
there hides a memory of man to illustrate."

"You are thinking," I said, "of Praxiteles, and beyond,
to that business of God's image, which is harmony
as measured by the famous scholastic hole

in Plato's head, where nothing is really real
but the abstraction of nothing—of the idea
of the abstraction of nothing—to an absolute.

After you, blessed maestro, came genre—the thing
measured not by absolutes but by other examples
of the same school. I am, alas, *that* man."

"Forgive me," he said, "I seem to hear you claim
an absolute irrelevance as a poor excuse
for what there's no excuse for." "None," I said,

"but a reverence for what was never there.
God measures perfection and crock measures pot."
—"You make me grateful I died in God's formed day."

"Master," I answered, "do you imagine God
is thinking you in this sequence? I'm
thinking you, more reverently, I daresay,

than He would be inclined to, were He inclined."
He looked away. "If I sense what you mean,
I am obliged to add that the thought disturbs me."

"Great Soul," I said, "how else could we have fallen
out of your circle but in that same disturbance
no man asked for and none yet has welcomed?"

"Thank you for a theme," he said. "I shall try
a drawing of it. If it lives on paper—
if I can make it live—I may understand."

"I wish I could hold to this same dream," I told him,
"Until it contains that drawing." "Perhaps," he said,
"it will be in one that comes later." "I will live for that,"

I said. But woke. The air was soup. The power still off.
It was pointless to try for sleep again in nature.
I went down and opened a bottle and sat to the dark.

UGLINESS

The windows I see into
when the El stops
are my hunchback cousin Sal
dead there
            the paint flaking

his pretty good tenor
gone under curve-screech
when he starts again being
one of the big kids
I was small to and always
glad faster
to see him come laughing.

When we had to find jobs
he couldn't lift anything
and ran numbers
darkened by cops
but went to night school
till he lit himself
a bookkeeper and a desk
to come from easy
again.

        And moved to New York
and nothing, the firm folding
and times tough those
years I hadn't seen him
and needed work and wrote me
—Sal, my goddamn beautiful
twisted own big brother cousin—
"Dear Mr. Ciardi. . . ."

                              And if I do not
cry into one of these
dead alley windows once,
what tear shall I ever
be some of a man to?

WASHING YOUR FEET

Washing your feet is hard when you get fat.

* * *

In lither times the act was unstrained and pleasurable.

* * *

You spread the toes for signs of athlete's foot.

* * *

You used creams, and rubbing alcohol, and you powdered.

* * *

You bent over, all in order, and did everything.

* * *

Mary Magdalene made a prayer meeting of it.

* * *

She, of course, was washing not her feet but God's.

* * *

Degas painted ladies washing their own feet.

* * *

Somehow they also seem to be washing God's feet.

* * *

To touch any body anywhere should be ritual.

* * *

To touch one's own body anywhere should be ritual.

* * *

Fat makes the ritual wheezy and a bit ridiculous.

* * *

Ritual and its idea should breathe easy.

* * *

They are memorial, meditative, immortal.

* * *

Toenails keep growing after one is dead.

* * *

Washing my feet, I think of immortal toenails.

* * *

What are they doing on these ten crimped polyps?

*   *   *

I reach to wash them and begin to wheeze.

*   *   *

I wish I could paint like Degas or believe like Mary.

*   *   *

It is sad to be naked and to lack talent.

*   *   *

It is sad to be fat and to have dirty feet.

KRANZFELDT

Kranzfeldt, the housepainter,
fell off more wagons in his time
than Texas has horses for.

His time up, he proceeded
to fall off the staging
at the Westmore, or fell off

without procedure, fracturing
more than would mend. Still
purposeful, he sent for whiskey

in the hope of dying closer
to the good of wanting. Fechner
the imbecile, left wet promises

but came back with Father Zingler
of the Society of Dry Reasons,
who offered a handful of dust.

I doubt I'll need all of God
for what happens next, but bring me
what's drinkable: I promise it thirst.

SMALL

Swatted a custardy small thing.
A stain with a shell center.
Ugh where its eyes were. This
I must dawdle at. What was it?
All of itself. Not much
of what I am. How much
of what I am not will stop
at my eyeholes leaking after?

Why dawdle at nothing left?
Ask God later. His last word
unsays the first. I am. This was.
What else have I to do
but watch what I can—
and while—asking it?
What's small enough
to stay wholly outside of?

And inside? In the eye
of custardy small things
is the universe other raisins
than heroes munch? What grades
the sensations of protein?
I'm ego and think questions;
dread, and guess answers
at stains of myself.

If I can be situation comedy
at last eyeholes,
let me speak good ironic lines
going from compassionate
disinterest to what small
cleaning problem will not

be there long enough
for much notice.

If it is a passion play
I must sink through, flailing
nerve ends like wires of a blown
still spinning computer,
tears of solder melting me
from connection, good lines lost
in the stink and peel of burning
till even fire's out—

then pity me, dawdlers, for your own sake,
that I was a man at the edge
of your interest, and within mine,
wanted no more than to go
toward custard from firm eyes,
quipping a final style
for what shapeless small wonder
we could have loved through.

A HEREAFTER

A sellspiel spitspray wordwind of a man
selfsold to every slogan on the board
loves me as God cannot, unless He can
sell me more safety than I can afford
and still eat daybread. Francis, to be sure,
put everything in insurance. I could sign,
eke out two selfless years among God's
    poor,
then blow my brains out on the dotted
    line
and be a saint in Probate. Or pass
    unchecked
by putting my body down in my wife's
    name.
Not even Francis, though he nearly
    wrecked
his father's business playing that saint's
    game
of give-away, so gave skin, blood, and
    bone
into the balance sheet of his Estate.
I could die rich so selflessly that none
could tax my memory.
                This sputter-spate
jargoning anagogue who speaks in
    tongues
that break before the Mystery, this oracle
of Tables from which Laws are struck
    like gongs
on great graphed peaks, this metaphorical
Father of Accountants leads me high
and spreads the world at my feet, all gold
    and awe

floating like heralds to my eye. And I
need only sign to be a saint at Law.

METAMORPHOSIS: THE PINK KNIGHT

A tic in the unreachable
flat of the back goads
the hero. It is madness
to itch so small. He *won't*
stop for it. Riding, he
writhes at what he
can't reach of himself. It
will pass
          but
               doesn't.
It
  is
    Cause
         finally
must
     wait.
            Dismounted,
unbuckled, bare to the waist,
a fair fool, he rubs
against shagbark. *Ah!*

But it won't stop. He
can't stop it. He scours
on the rasp, guesses he
is bleeding. What rapture
agony is! He damns his
horse for nothing, for
grazing easy and brutal.
The tree's a hot grate.
He blackens like steak
stuck to it and can't
pull off. Skin and his
vows shred. He learns

pleasure that can't be
ended. Ever?
                One
lucid time later
he finds a girl from
the village standing
there, a basket-
headed cow-slut
laughing—she dares
to. It burns. He
burns. He is sinking
into the tree afire,
A fire laughing. He
can,
        too.
                Dares
                        to.
Damn
        her
                vows
                        Cause.
Ah!
        a breeze slips
from flags he leaves.
A sending. Ascending. He
leaves with it, uprushing,
brims over and still
rises. His leaves quake,
signal like heliographs,
a sundance explodes,
his horse bolts thunder,
the slut gibbers to
arms and knees under him
praying at the feet of
his leaking red godhead.

And still rising.
                Ah!

EAST SIXTY-SEVENTH STREET

Wondering what to take seriously
without going as far as Fire Island,
I sit with Jamie to suffer his fourth bar.

Frank O'Hara died there, X'd out
by a beach buggy, its tire-tread scrawled
like a moustache on a poster. Let it not be

Fire Island. There could be another cause
not to die of. Maybe a liberation
from too much fretting. "We are so damned worthless!"

sighs Jamie the assessor. The universe
owes him a meaning. His mother, a Jewish princess
with an ark in her cleft, taught him to expect:

See my apple? It's from the Hesperides.
You could never imagine such fruit!
—No, nor distinguish it from another.

Now, having bitten it and found it mealy,
he can't get through the night on less than six
bars to his grief, some of which could be real,

maybe enough to mourn a meaning for handsome
Frank O'Hara, my student and friend once,
his headfull leaking into a tire track

on the sands of the gay. Whatever it comes to.
As Jamie might be suffering not to suffer
but because we are what we are and some of it hurts.

AN APOLOGY FOR NOT INVOKING THE MUSE

Erato popped in. What a talent for suspicion!
"Now what?" she said. I thought I knew.
"I am writing an unimportant poem," I told her.

She slammed her lute down on my desk.
Slammed it so hard it shook the air forever.
Even in anger she gives off such sounds

I cannot summon an adequate emotion
except in sensing how all loss belittles
what's left to make a truth of.

"Who authorized that?" she wanted to know.
"Honey," I said, "do I have to check with you
before I scratch an itch? This was a small one

in a minor crease I needn't specify
except to say we all have some—I mean
we mortals—and they do burn."

Was I being unreasonable? She chose to wail.
"Four thousand years of lute lessons in those crags
in a suffered dream of tuning types like you,

and you show your gratitude by scratching creases!"
—Nothing is more demanding than a woman
who has given everything. Yet, how she glowed!

"Darling," I said, "you were born to natural grandeur.
I worship you for it. Gratefully. I've prayed
to be worthy of you. It's no use:

"I am small, dull, subject to gravity, and locked
in these creases that itch and must be scratched
by those who haven't had your advantages.

"Besides—may I add?—this unimportant poem
is outbulging Doric proportion. Less
would be better than more, being more to the fact."

She glared nobility. "Are you one of mine,
and still dare speak of unimportant poems?
The least song, clod, consumes the singer!"

"Angel," I pleaded, "not everything's an *Aeneid*—
which would make it Calliope's business, to begin with. . . ."
She flatted: "You leave my sister out of this!"

"I mean, I love you most for the sweet small
that trembles to a silence it awakens
and echoes back a ghost, when you let me say it."

"*I* let you say it! You didn't even invoke me!
You haven't invoked me in over forty years!"
I recalled my first trembling toward her and burned with
    shame.

"Beloved," I said, "I didn't want to bother you.
I thought I could say this little on my own,
the way it happens to us in our smallness."

She touched a chord and was herself again—
I have never seen her more glorious—then leaned down
to read what I had written, then stood tall.

"See for yourself what comes of that!" she said,
and struck her lute and was gone wherever she goes
to the silence trembling after her. In silence

I read what I had written, and despaired.
How had I dared imagine I might dare
be only what I am?
     and yet . . .
       and yet . . . .

A FOOL TOO FAST

A fool too fast, his taillights dwindling
into the heavy footed dream he goes great
leaves red fur on the lawn—dog-kindling
from the stumps of an easy love, and Kate
in a rag statuary of pathos kneeling
to tears she does not know are ordinary.
"Dodo! Oh, Dodo!" She might be Job keening
"What is my guilt?"—as if this earth, this bestiary
of reasonably simple motives were at its first
and every emotion notable. Ah, but she feels
what we only know: the shock and thrust
of what might as easily not have happened, of wheels
so fast they blurstill but leavedead
what Kate can't learn to ask nor father nor school
answer of how tears are shed,
and then grief, but not the unstoppable fool.

ONE WET IOTA

I could see God once when I believed telling
look into a mud and His eye
start one wet iota swelling.

An untold later toward some when and why
come to no answer, I put
a lesson to a lens and saw the jelly

webbed to bone-spars of a live frog's foot
flow like blips across a radar screen.
And that was all blood circling in and out.

Told or untold, I saw nothing mean
but small looking. I can look home
to the size God was, seeing the thing seen

start like that wet iota and become.

HISTORY IS WHAT A MAN DOES

History is what a man does
entering a friend's house, and what he thinks
doing it. It is the right of the youngest son
against the eldest. It is written
in the answers he gives a beggar while guessing
that the man is needy or a professional,
and then in musing that need, too, is a profession.

These are advanced stages. It starts
by deciding which men shall be on a man's side
in the killing of others. All who join a man
in the killing he does are brothers
and holy; all others, "barbarians,"
the word meaning at once "strangers" and "enemies."

In ritual, then, manners become laws;
laws, religions; and religions,
institutions and administrations. Much depends
on how many battles are won and lost;
even more, on which. After climactic killing
comes peace, tilled by slaves. Commerce
and philosophy become famous handicrafts.

Uncomfortably, there remain the free citizens
too poor to own slaves, forbidden
to till like slaves, and not immediately
needed for the army. Still brothers
and ritual, they are your reserve
for the next killing. They must be fed
and amused and you must pretend to honor them.

They do have the old claim their fathers
had on yours while killing together,
and it does outlast generations. In the end

it becomes just too damned expensive.
Mercenaries are cheaper, probably better,
and need not be consulted as if votes mattered.
Money is the new government,

the poor are criminals, and criminals,
once caught and sentenced, are slaves.
It's so easy you grasp instantly
your fathers were fools for not seeing it.
At that point, inevitably, religion changes
again. Ritual has already changed.
And you have thirty ships at sea

bringing home spices, rhinoceros horn, slaves,
and more change. Your cousin
loses a castle a day for two months
at dice. You conclude he's no good
but blood remains an obligation:
you lend him your dirk to kill himself,
and have a good artist do his tomb.

The next day, entering a friend's house,
you discover he, too, is bankrupt.
After lending him less than you spent
on your last whore, you goose his wife.
The pitiful bastard goes rhetorically
for his dagger. Your thugs cut his throat.
His wife, simpering, asks you into her bath.

By now the slaves are sullen. Pirates
take two ships. Then six. The mercenaries
demand payment. Eight more ships are lost.
The mercenaries throw in with the barbarians.
The slaves set fire to the harvest.
Horsemen ride in from the north haggard,
interrupting even the loveliest orgies.

You take to your last castle,
luckily an island with unassailable cliffs.
In two years you're down to your own
sour wine, goat's milk, and mealy olives.
Someone else's ships sail by you.
You watch and grow older. Your son
forms a band of boys who will kill with him.

They go out in boats and come in with plunder.
One great axe-clanging oaf
brings you a jug of real Falerno
but trips, drops it, and the jug shatters
with your cup and tongue both out.
You raise the cup to bash his skull,
and your son knocks it from your hand.

"We have stood together, he and I,
and killed together. If this is my house,
no man may offend him in it.
If it is not my house, it cannot stand."
You know then how old you are.
"Are there beggars at the gate?" you ask.
"Here," he tells you, "there are no beggars."

A pity. They would have been something
to join: a thought, and none to take it;
understanding, and none to speak it to.
You remember that your father is dead,
and his father, and your son another man.
And what man are you, who cannot remember
to the nearest province what you spent on whores?

MEMOIR OF A THREE INCH MAN

I did no more than mention to the witch doctor
that he seemed to be taking with full seriousness
what existed, if at all,
only on questionable evidence.

I knew, of course, he had been ordained.
I had seen his certificate of election
to both houses, his brevet as a brigadier,
the empowering resolution appointing him
Head of Judiciary, and I had heard him
refuse the Presidency three times.

I was, therefore, prepared,
for the authority of his damnation.

What I could not believe
till my clothes began folding in on me
was the actual shrinkage of tissue.

2:00 A.M.

I was bleeding checks at the dining room table—
Bell Tel., Elec-Gas, Wilentz & Wilentz
(for court appearance, pot bust, 16 April),
plus orthodontia, lawn care, my inalienable
taxes, real and personal—dollars and cents
to the edge of balance (which I have never yet)
and beyond to the phone jangling from outer space
that the world is overdrawn and I'd best get
material witnesses down or lose my case

when

like a reassertion of the unpayable wind
an ocelot's ear fell flush on "Ex-act-illy
One Thousand Five Hundred to K. J. Susskind,
DDS." Oh, jungle! A tiger lily
from the centerpiece my wife had flamed in a vase
for her ladies' luncheon-gaggle and sherry-swozzle
had puckered loose and witnessed, changing the case.
I may win it after all. Not even Judge Fossil
can overrule the revelations of fauna,
the descent of omens to Abraham & Strauss,
of testaments to Am. Ex., demonstrable manna
to Raritan Oil Co., ever sufficient grace
to N. J. Mortagage, tidings of good cheer
to D & L Liquors, and to Claery & Dietz,
Tree Surgeons, for staying my elm another year,
the annunciation of the triumphant beast.

A THANKS TO A BOTANIST

Setting his camera to blink a frame
every X minutes, his lights to a forcing pace,
he shot a reel of growth from seed to sere.
The Half Hour of the Zinnia. Up it rode,
slippering toward light, sliding from swelling pockets,
unfurling flowering hands from ends of thread,
holding them up to light, then letting fall,
and threads fall: a river system fled backward
to no system. Has God seen this
His distance from all fact? A man and camera
passed the miracle of the raised usual
and brought this near-weed to motion
and counter-motion. As music is—
an ecology of idea in balance.

Could a tree grow in thirty
held minutes of such blinking, that
would be a visible symphony.

ON THE ORTHODOXY AND CREED OF
MY POWER MOWER

All summer in power, outroaring the bull fiend,
    it raves on my lawn, spewing
into the dirty lung hung on its side.
    Myself maddened by power, I ride
the howl of hot new-mown sacks-full,
    the powder bursts of gnashed mole runs,
till in one sweaty half day of the beast
    my lawn is lined to tidy passages. So
neatness from lunacy, the orderliness of rage,
    Bedlam's Eden, all calm now,
the dead beast washed in cool light and stalled.

Again and again, all summer in power at a touch,
    it frenzies. At fall's dry last
I kneel to the manual, to the word, touch,
    and pour extreme unctions that the locked life
waken when called. And do call, year after year
    in season, to the lunacy of power and am not answered.
I probe, prime, pump, and might as well pray
    to headless stone gods. Nothing—
nothing I know—wakens the power blast
    hidden in it, which is no cause of protestant
conscience to be worked out between me and the source
    but a priest-held power of maintenance.

Always at last defeated, I call, and its priest comes
    with cups, knowledge, and the anointed touch
that does reach power and mystery. The beast
    gasps, shakes, wavers deep in itself, then
roars full to resurrection, and here we come
    to cure green again, our triumph of faith!
Which is, of course, that even the powerless

and inept may ride fit power once wakened
by the anointed man believed in
   deeper than conscience and defeat;
whole in his knowledge given, his touch charged,
   the dangerous blind beast tame in service.

TO A LOVELY LADY GONE TO THEORY

You could be the beginning of treated birds
that have changed their migration patterns.

Doctor Tinker has found the code written
on the inner wall of the egg and transcribed it.

Now he can read it, but the birds can't.
Some of them start south again every Tuesday.

When I come home too fast then, my scrambler
jamming the State Police radar,

they hear my wave length as a mating signal
and light on my roof, drunk with a wrong nisus.

You wouldn't entirely believe what happens
in the jungle gym of my T.V. antenna.

Then, in a week, the weighted egg yet to come,
their new signal scrambles them south again.

Some of them. Many, I know, do not make it.
Some no longer balance on the air.

I find bodies in the driveway. Or my mower
sprays them. I no longer drive on Tuesdays

for fear of calling them or the State Cops.
I depend on cabs and on having nowhere to go.

On Wednesday, when I find you there, we are both
littered with dead birds. Is there no end to them?

They keep on coming faster than they die.
Then they keep dying almost as fast as they come.

Sometimes they sing as if all were well again.
I am tempted to doubt what I know about them. And us.

Always then it comes Tuesday again and it starts;
Wednesday, and once more I know what I know.

Sooner or later, I see, I must give you up
to that tireless Doctor who meddles with everything.

Go to him: finish building your faith around him.
I have had enough of watching us go random,

everything responding but in no sequence.

IN THE HOLE

I had time and a shovel. I began to dig.
There is always something a man can use a hole for.
Everyone on the street stopped by. My neighbors
are purposeful about the holes in their lives.
All of them wanted to know what mine was *for*.

Briggs asked me at ten when it was for the smell
of new-turned sod. Ponti asked at eleven
when it was for the sweat I was working up.
Billy LaDue came by from school at one
when it was for the fishing worms he harvested.

My wife sniffed in from the Protestant ethic at four
when the hole was for finding out if I could make
a yard an hour. A little after five
a squad car stopped and Brewster Diffenbach,
pink and ridiculous in his policeman suit,

asked if I had a building permit. I told him
to run along till he saw me building something.
He told me I wasn't being cooperative.
I thanked him for noticing and invited him
to try holding his breath till he saw me change.

I ate dinner sitting on its edge. My wife
sniffed it out to me and sniffed away.
She has her ways but qualifies—how shall I say?—
alternatively. I'd make it up to her later.
At the moment I had caught the rhythm of digging.

I rigged lights and went on with it. It smelled
like the cellar of the dew factory. Astonishing

how much sky good soil swallows. By ten-thirty
I was thinking of making a bed of boughs at the bottom
and sleeping there. I think I might have wakened

as whatever I had really meant to be once.
I could have slept that close to it. But my wife
came out to say nothing whatever, so I showered
and slept at her side after making it up to her
as best I could, and not at all bad either.

By morning the hole had shut. It had even
sodded itself over. I suspect my neighbors.
I suspect Diffenbach and law and order.
I suspect most purposes and everyone's
forever insistence I keep mine explainable.

I wish now I had slept in my hole when I had it.
I would have made it up to my wife later.
Had I climbed out as I had meant to be—
really meant to be—I might have really
made it up to her. I might have unsniffed her

clear back to dew line, back to how it was
when the earth opened by itself and we
were bared roots.—Well, I'd had the exercise.
God knows I needed it and the ache after
to sing my body to sleep where I remembered.

And there *was* a purpose. This is my last house.
If all goes well, it's here I mean to die.
I want to know what's under it. One foot more
might have hit stone and stopped me, but I doubt it.
Sand from an old sea bottom is more likely.

Or my fossil father. Or a mud rosary.
Or the eyes of the dog I buried south of Jerusalem

to hide its bones from the Romans. Purpose
is what a man uncovers by digging for it.
Damn my neighbors. Damn Brewster Diffenbach.

KEEPING

Put a dog in a bottle. It won't bark.
Not long. A scuba diver can't. He'll
swim up to the cork and try knifing it.
He has about thirty minutes to knife through.
Sometimes, for the strongest, that's enough.
If, therefore, you really mean
to keep things bottled, do not fill to the top.
It may be better to use no liquids at all.
Some ferment and blow the cork.
Any of them makes the bottle heavy
and the act of bottling up is itself
heavy enough. Suppose you were to spend
all your nights for years building a ghost ship
or a replica of your nervous system
inside the bottle, then filled it with water:
unless you used some nonbiodegradable
plastic junk, the thing would waterlog
and turn to bloat. If it didn't disintegrate
it would run, leaving you a dirty bottle.
It is nuisance enough to carry the thing around
without having to watch it go dirty.
Not that you can manage without one.
You have yours. I have mine. We all
have something to put into it. Does it matter
what? We aren't given much choice.
Often, as I sense it, we have nothing to do
with actually doing it. We look,
and there is the bottle with things in it—
the dog, for example, that stopped barking
instantly its forty years ago
but starts again unstopped the instant we look
and remember there is the bottle, and what's in it.

4:00 A.M. THE BOTTLE IS A CLEPSYDRA

A preacher I left in California
used to sweat through his pants when God came heavy.
His Sundays read the same backward and forward,
but religion is something to do. At first light
I took the basket and went out for the eggs
we would go to God on. Buzz-buzz be His flies.
A henhouse, mother, is a stinking convent,
but we'll have holy breakfast. "Ouef! Ouef! Ouef!"
said Sartre the French poodle, lifting his leg
on a weed he was misnaming till it scolded:
"Camus saw I was sumac!" I am myself
part of a palindrome of my weedy fathers
under the raised leg of my neighbor's shadow.
His wife has a mole I will not mention to him.
Would he believe extenuating circumstances?
Law is man's guilty conscience codified.
Like the phone book, it's no guest list. Never invite
what you don't want an answer from. Here are the eggs
mother is waiting for. I have wiped them with hay,
knowing she keeps a fastidious kitchen, at least
till the San Andreas fault is re-edited.
The crockery from her shelves will do for footnotes
if there's a page left or a thing to explain.
What matters is the way we choose what matters.
Or are chosen. Or find in the flower bed under the window
a footprint with no heelmark is a plot.
Everyone's in it—preacher, mother, Sartre,
San Andreas—but there is no necessary
connection between most things and most others.
The look of the world is in the way it is looked at.
This bottle is a clepsydra and has run out.

BLUE MOVIE

There is no cause for love in such a script,
nor even for much transition. Two girls come
mincing in crinoline to a pool. Stripped
as if on truant impulse, frolicsome
(the camera zooming in on clefts and hair),
they wet a toe and show the water's cold
by hugging one another in play, till bare
touch to bare touch tingles, and they fold

together on the moss bank and lie panting.
Their white hams, like their hamming, twitch and tremble
till teasing teases something like true wanting.
Not all of even this flesh can dissemble.
Some part of false touch touches. Thighs outflung
to camera angles, they squirm public meat
till they are tongue to crotch and crotch to tongue,
their bellies beaded wet in a made heat.

Cut to two lordly hunters in the wings,
a camera on their flies, which they unzip
with that same cueing from the first of things
that says, "No introductions, boys. Just strip."
And *ooh* and *aah*, the maidens (only started
by girlish mere contrivance) flit away
behind a bush. (No, they have not departed:
they run to show the cameras what will stay.)

The hunters and their finger-beckoned bunnies
wet one another. For such juices once
the gods came down. Now, retold in the funnies,
Leda and Europa, two coy cunts,
having been spread and had, work up to tricks.
Drooling at the boys' crotches all a-wiggle,

they beg the unwilted gods, and those rock pricks
pump their assholes while the humped girls giggle.

There, while mythologies teach them their Greek,
they French kiss like two chums at boarding school.
The camera, in a high artistic streak
flashes a hot montage of ass, tit, tool,
the kissing girls, and their ooh-la-la eyes.
Enter, of course, two other hunters then —
it's the quail season. Still quick to surprise,
the girls, still bashful, hug and cry, "Ooh — men!"

The rest is variations of no art
at easy orifices, one by one,
and two by two. A shock of flesh to start,
then bald redundancy. In tireless fun
the flesh assembles, joins, and then untangles
to start again, stretched skins of pure intent.
Their one lie is that nothing ever dangles
but outyearns Keats, in spending still unspent.

Till the director, bored to the point of wit,
works up a last touch. When the hunters go,
still cocky after twelve dives in the pit,
he shows the broads arranged in a tableau
of innocence undone by bestial rape.
Strewn like husks and separate on their bed
of swallowing moss, they sink to dark and gape
the disassembled gestures of the dead.

THE MAGICIAN

"Watch closely," he said, palming the word "God"
then opening both hands empty, then reaching
to snatch it from the air with a sword through it,
then turning it over to show it changed to "History."
which he dropped into his hat. "Now," he said,
picking up his wand, "what will you have back?"
"Justice," I said, improvising. He tapped
and skulls began brimming over to roll on the stage.
"Aspiration!" I cried to stop him. He tapped more skulls.
"No," I cried. "Love!" He tapped and still they came.
"Purpose!" Tap-tap. "Loyalty!" Tap-tap.
"Mankind!" At every tap the dead came grinning.
I understood — was it part of his illusion? —
that these were all who had killed one another
for high cause, being at least partly selfless
in their reasons. "Who would have killed in any case,"
the illusion corrected, "but were more comfortable
once they had installed reasons upon their motives."
"Reason, then!" I cried. He put the hat on,
telescoped the wand, which he put in his pocket,
and waved the skulls to gas, the vapor lifting
from a bare and dirty stage, and he gone from it.

DIFFERENCES

Choose your own difference between surgery
and knifing. Both cut. One
thinks to rejoin. Can something be made
of this difference? Defend your answer.

Now think of a surgery without intention:
here the scalpels, there the body.
Everyone is some doctor. You, too,
may as well be employed. Cut.

Is this something like a soft version
of a machine built to do nothing?
We are experimenting in the new art:
by contradicting purpose we explore.

possibly nothing, but explore,
possibly a reality, possibly a way
of inventing what a reality might be
had we some way of inventing it.

The first incision is hardest, but look
closely: you will find it already made,
inherent. Put the alarm clock inside it
and stitch. You now have a TV commercial

someone could be born to or die of.
And you? Are you my murderer
or my healer? You do know. Why else
did you set the alarm without being told?

Remember, however: distinctions
are never made wholly for their own sake.

You are doomed to decide not only
what you do but what you have done.

Yes, we chose what was already open,
putting into it what came to hand.
We must still take what attitude we can
toward what will already have been done

by the time we have time to think about it.
Were we successful killers or failed
surgeons? We will come to that difference.
And what difference will it make?

A BUDDHA SEEN AS THE THING LEAST LIKE ME

Bangkok, 1967

So then, to Buddha's blazing cave,
lit ornament by ornament
to vaults of gold. What a tall grave
an idea is! Sky, be my tent.
I have a day a tourist bought,
this blind look of outlasted thought,

and that untraceable slow smile
that may, in some eternity,
reach to a laugh, but meanwhile—
conceived as a serenity—
draws back from everything man is.
How could he hold his mood, like this,

a century in, a century out,
then a millennium, then again,
and still again? and never doubt
time enough will still remain
to hold it and let it go?
so, so, so, so, so, so, and so?

"Carved in the living rock . . . ." What's that?—
a guide book phrase? When shall rock live?
Carved in the living lean and fat,
blood, bone, and nerve sieve
that sifts idea like the rock chips
whose falling leaves the Buddha's lips

in what was only blank and stone.
A totem-top where mountain was.
A blind god looking down alone
thinking what anthills in His grass

we think Him from, this tourist-bought
blind day of our outlasted thought.

LETTER FROM A PANDER

Nothing, the cross-haired sky tells lenses,
is long. A flare behind Arcturus
reaches how far? It's over. There is
this while of days, eras, species
between novas. And that guessed
machine of bursts—does it burst, too?
Sooner ask doctoral gnats
their theory of evolution:
no scale speaks another.

"Eternal City," says the myth-nerve:
a twinge of self, long to that scale
invisible to another. "Immortal Homer,"
says Liberal Arts: a cultural eternity,
two shelves of the fissionable library.
And the infinities of the Etruscans?
—who speaks them on what scale?
what did those lovers do
to be forgotten in a lost tongue?

"Countless as stars in the sky,"
sang the rhapsode, whose naked eye
never saw more than fifteen hundred at once
had he thought to count them
the clearest night of his evanescence.
What liars poets are! Toward,
I suppose, some nerve-truth,
could they find it to say, as some—
all the good ones—have.

                    Yet fogged.
One squirt of mother's milk in the eye
and we're blinded. We suck

nonsense with love, then defend
love *and* nonsense. And say
we endure millennia — will we have learned?

Do not hurry the answer.
We are newer than newts here.
Could the race learn its scale,
a greatness — something like
a greatness on some
scale we might agree on our while —
seems possible. Remember
love itself may be madness.
But where then is the child's milk?
and the man? and millennium come to?

We may also blow ourselves out of whiles
this reasoned step by step we go blam.

Now then, toward neither nonsense
nor always, and on no scale
we are finally sure of, can you
in the soft transcience and girl-dusk
of what could be instantly
your nakedness, think better access
to this moon's rising?
                    Off
with propositions, darling. I speak
a fathering disinterest. I set these lines
for a boy to say to you
toward his Now and yours
on their own scale.
                    Answer softly.
It is gentleness forgives us.
Refuse him if he is dull, but not
because he will not love you always.
Nor you, him.

If authorities
question you later, tell them
a dead man was your pander,
and loved you as God should.

NOTES

I found myself at the conceptual tomb
of Saint Theresa with no particular
intention. I had been browsing
and it caught my attention.

At once I began to develop attitudes,
expectations. "Here I am,"
I said to myself on p. 1,
"approaching the conceptual tomb."

I sensed I might be about to enter
some centralizing experience. The presence of even
conceived absolutes is rare and powerful.
It was, I found, the absolute that shifted.

"God-rayed, god-blinded, god-taken
sub-Immaculata of the direct experience,"
I noted in the margin of p. 32,
"I feel you turning into observed data."

"Epitome," I concluded on p. 402,
"something is forever red-kneed kneeling
in chosen gravels I have no cartilage for.
Thank you for the notes I have taken."

"What's at the bottom of one pecking order
could, with intelligence, fantasize another,"
I wrote on p. 77 of a later notebook
on the behavior of lesser apes I was

imitating for data in the crotch-cramping saddle
of a tree of patience, the replacement batteries
in my left cheek pocket martyring
my unadapted metaphysical ass.

Is it purposeful, I wonder, to endure this
stumped straddle of observation posts,
the gouging of what equips us,
the banality of recorded impressions?

Hanged (experimentally) from the same tree
I held my breath to watch the snorting ecstasy
of mating hippopotami. I would have exhaled
saeculi saeculorum but for the rope

and the thought that I might hang there
unannotated—which moved me to seize the branch,
climb back to my notebook, and slip off
the parachute harness I had been faking it with.

They had plowed the ground under me. There was blood
on the female's back—even for hippos
it is a tearing weight. They have gone off
in different directions. If something

is born of this, it will repeat itself
to extinction, or to mutation and then extinction.
Between itself and whatever comes last
there will be experiences and they should be noted.

DRIVING ACROSS THE AMERICAN DESERT
AND THINKING OF THE SAHARA

I hang the cloth water bag from the door mirror.
A seepage evaporates. By wasting a little,
and having a wind to my going, I cool—
almost to freshness — what I live by.

I cross bone dusts to rimrock,
leaving a storm of dust in my rear vision.
I breathe some million molecules of argon
breathed by Christ once. Part of His pronunciation.

The dust of saints' brain cells is also a matter of fact.
I rinse it from my throat, let the water bag swing to the wind,
its strap tilting the mirror to sky. I adjust it
back to the storm I make and forever leave.

At sundown in an oasis of green money
girls silvery as frost on pewter goblets
smile me from passage to a made air,
time and space filtered from it.

I pay gladly for absolution
from saints' grit, rimrock, the sucking sun
burning the storm I stirred and outran
the other side of this filter we change through

from what lies open, where any man
can feel his immortalities sucked like water
to gather and fall again—and who knows where?—
till even the sun we can bear some of

gasps; and it, unchangeable argon, bone dust,
saint dust, dust of the last idea,

drift wide gravities that will—somewhere
outside dens we come to—form again.

REQUISITIONING

> *I needed 800 dozen golf balls.*
> *I got 1700 basketball hoops.*
> — From an advertisement by Western Electric

There are no imperfect answers from perfect data.

Spec numbers, state of Inventory-Now,
urgency of requirement as crosshatched
from orders outstanding, credit substantiation,
promised delivery plus days of grace,
seasonal-demand configuration
adjusted for such variables as weather,
shifts in population, inductive events
(the sales effect, for example, of opening day
of the baseball season), duration of induction,
disposable income, demographic doctrine
— all must be weighed where all things balance true.

The answers are beyond us, not the method.
We describe our need, submitting it as we know it,
laboring always for the perfected input.

The Circuits then decide. We may think, at first,
they ignore our need. In time we understand
they scan that total universe of data
that is not visible to us at our stations.

We think we need 800 dozen golf balls:
good faith has been tendered, the customer confirmed,
we get back 1700 basketball hoops
and the customer phones for redemption: rains
have flooded the courses, the play has moved indoors,
gyms are under construction everywhere:

the need is for 3000 basketball hoops
with nets, backboards, brackets.
                              We absolve him
and send up the conversion. We get back
5000 pairs of water skis — regular, slalom,
trick, a few with hydroplanes. — Of course!
the flooding has been calculated. Seepage
has warped the gym floors. Cancel basketball.

We learn to answer as we are willed to answer
where all our needs are known before we know them
and ministered to our good.

                              There are, to be sure,
those 1700 basketball hoops, now surplus,
but before we can remainder them, Public Works
sends in an order for them as mooring rings.

That, too, as we see backwards, was foreseen.

There in the total universe of data
all things are parts and harmonies of one plan
that calls us to Itself, demanding only
our faith and our vocation to describe
fallibly, but laboring for perfection,
the need that shall be given perfect answers.

NOTES FROM THE SYSTEM

I was not thinking of myself.
I had already escaped the system.
In return for reciting prepared testimony
against my mother and your father,
most of which was, anyhow, true—
or will turn out to be
once we are broken to honesty—
I had been given my belt back
and was free to hang myself
as soon as I could put my neck in order.

Yet even as I sat savoring my escape
I would see a glow from the dark corner
and Innocenza would have her halo
turned on again. "Man," I told myself,
"must still be capable of a last purity."
It became my holy obsession
not to die till Innocenza was free.

Can faith pick locks? I could no longer
have endured for myself
the shapelessness of freedom.
Yet, living a fiction, I imagined.
What was too much for my senses
was the least I could offer
my own idea of radiance.
She also had nice tits,
and I liked to imagine someone
not even aware of what he owed me
fumbling the good of them, as the best
is always wasted on fumblers.

I was in no way bitter
about the ineptitude of boys

who get the best, even when
they mistake it for the ordinary.
How else do we live? For me
it was enough to make a last lost cause
of the continuity of possible good.

Something will pick locks, if only
the jailor, and all jailors,
like all prisoners, can be bribed.
Wisdom is the art of knowing
what bribe will move the given jailor.

I studied, made pigments from soot,
bird's blood, and pollen; painted
a four dimensional Pietà
on both sides of my starched
underwear. "In New York,"
I told the jailor, "Parke Bernet
could sell it to Norton Simon
for six million." The jailor
looked in his book. "I have no visa."

On my last shirt
I wrote 47 symphonies
in dodecatonic accelerations beyond
pitch but transferable through prisms
into light patterns that guarantee orgasm
even to the three months dead.
"You don't know my wife," said the jailor.

I tried all seven arts and invented
seven more. My socks and handkerchiefs
went, then my shoes. I was down
to pantaloons. Nothing was art enough
for the peasant with a key. "And still,"
I told him, "there must be a price
for anything." "Of course,"

he said, picking his nose
"What were you thinking of buying?"

The next day the commissioner
of information came by on his clipboard.
"Speak sotto voce," he said.
"I have the notation." — "Innocenza,"
I whispered, "my life for hers
if need be." — "Everything's possible,"
he yawned, and wrote on himself.

The next day the procurator of physical
education came by with the commissioner
clipped to another clipboard
with all notations entered. "What,"
he said, "is your last offer?"
— "Whatever you ask." He read his notes.
"You have given your drawers for painting,
your shirt for music, your miscellany
for miscellaneous. Now to hit bottom:
will you drop your pants for mercy?"

I had been jailed here long enough
to understand at once. Alas,
I had not been jailed here long enough
to remember. "Beast!" I shrieked,
"Filthy beast! Decadent myrmidon!"

That night Innocenza was summoned.

My next day's meal was a thigh bone
on which was scratched: "Find the halo."

That night they took my belt back.
Now my pants fall by themselves.

Everything in the system learns the system.

EXIT LINE

Love should intend realities. Goodbye.

A CONFESSION: THAT I MEANT TO SING AND DID NOT

The interpreter was court appointed
without benefit of idiom. I understood
after some garlicky paragraphs of pidgin
he was asking, "How do you plead?"

I do not understand why I thought of my dog
in the first snow of his puppyhood
great-circling energy, an elation
to blood-root of the re-excited world.

Was it memory I must defend? I had been born,
there had been a world for running, I ran it.
Running was the first father gift. Running
and the sweat after running—a Christmas

of wound-up impulses in a skin stocking.
I ran like the dog my first time far:
it was Maine one morning, the world unreeling
habitats of dazzling autumn, the sun

prismed through apple bursts and chrome birch,
the dog's bliss of self so close to his blood
this earth could not have happened
but to quiver him there to the trance of himself.

I looked at the judge in his dead languages,
at the cracked statuary in the jury box.
The interpreter was still reciting
a bad breath I could not understand

except by guessing from bone contexts.
How should I plead? That I had not run enough?
Or had once, but lost the habit?
Had I bought the dog to run for me one winter

after Christmas and its empty stockings?
"Guilty," I said to the first kangaroo that dawn.
It was a whisper. "Guilty," I said to the herds
stampeding dusts from the Serengeti Plain.

"Guilty," I said in Boston, strolling the Common
when a pavement of pigeons broke, beating me
with their wings in one of the wind tunnels
where I was flight-tested and failed.

"There is," I said, "no consequence. This court
can confuse my idiom. It cannot say me."
Some stinking paragraphs later I understood
I had been sentenced to this reverie.

DIALOGUE WITH OUTER SPACE

Do you?
    Yes.
        Do you what?
            Whatever—
to the unqualified question the unqualified answer:
I do.
    Everything?
        Yes.
            Every*thing?*
                I do.
In the fact or the thought of it—everything.
What is done in fact without thought, in place of
thought. What is done thoughtfully, premeditatively
in fact. Or in thought only, to escape fact,
to make it bearable, to seduce it—everything.
And do you now confess?
                To myself, everything.
To the world in practical fact what is in its own terms
convenient. Except that in an anger like an assault
of honesty I do now and then not care and do openly
admit being and having been and meaning to be everything,
and to relive it.
        You have lied?
                I recall that life.
Cheated?
    And that one.
        Stolen?
            Negligently.
What has there been that would have been worth the time
it would have taken to steal it?
        But you have?
Sometimes there was something?
        At times. A trifle.

And always instantly not worth keeping.
You have killed?
        Always alas for the wrong reasons.
For what reasons?
         For duty. For my captain's approval.
Not for survival?
        Survival lay with my captain,
the controls his. I killed because I could.
You were proud?
        For no reason I have not survived.
Envious?
      At times, but I have admired many.
Wrathful?
        In bursts from the sperm center. A screeing
of sensation like Morse Code drowned in a cosmic whine.
Slothful?
      Yawningly when that was my mood's pleasure.
Avaricious?
     No.
        Gluttonous?
           Hungry.
            Lustful?
             Gladly.
What then do you believe should be done with your soul?
Erase its name and make way for another experience.
Why?
    First, because it is completed and time is not.
And second?
      Because it will in any case be erased.
And third?
      Because, though it does not matter, eternity
would be the one experience beyond mercy.
And you claim mercy?
      I do.
      Why?
        Because I was born.

GENERATION GAP

A PRAYER TO THE MOUNTAIN

Of the electric guitar as a percussion instrument
and of my son who wails twelve hours an animal day
in the stoned cellar of my house I sing, oh pot-head baby
from the rock rolled Nine Sisters classic crag group
hit album featuring The Body Counts in "I'm Blowing it Now"
from "Don't Have to Have a Reason till I Stop."

And pray to you, Apollo, first of indulgent fathers
to weep a thunderstruck son down from the high hots
on more horsepower than God could let run
and not fear. And also as the angel who backed
The Nine Sisters to all-time superstardom
on warehouses full of gold millionth albums
and a tax structure that could have saved England.

As you watched Daedalus once watch his boy down
from a high beyond warning, watched and remembered Phaeton
trailing a sky-scar, watched the man watch,
his eyes wind-watered but holding himself to flight-trim,
balancing slow cold turns down the hot shaft
the boy plunged, and hover at last too late
over the placeless water that had taken and closed . . .

Grant us, father, not a denial of energy,
its space-trip spree above environment,
but a rest of purposes after the seized seizure,
the silence after the plunge without the plunge,
a fulfillment not necessarily final,
an excursion not from but to one another.
—I ask as a son in thy son's name for my son.

A POEM FOR BENN'S GRADUATION FROM HIGH SCHOOL

Whenever I have an appointment to see the assistant
principal about my son again, if they will keep
him (which no one wants to and sometimes I)
it is always at 9:00 impossible o'clock A.M.

It is at least twenty years since I made it to
9:00 unbearable o'clock A.M. from the south side of sleep.
My one way there is the polar route over the Late Late
hump of the swozzled world's chain-smoking fog.

I do not seek these differences between me and
assistant whomevers. I am confined to them. Bit
by bit the original wiring of my nervous system
has been converted to solid state insomnia.

It does no good now to reverse the leads or to try
reprinting the circuits. At 9:00 paralyzed o'clock
A.M., in the name of what can despair and still
attend, I nod to the repetitions of the assistant

whomness. We are both dull as the Mudville choir
flatting platitudes. I could by now have been drunk,
enough possibly to doze. I do not need
to be stoned sleepless to know this boy is

difficult but more possible than this assistant
who-bah brisking me to ideal endeavor, community
cooperation, and the general detritus of the white
man's burden after the wreck of the Hesperus and

the spread of the Dutch Elm Beetle, which floated
ashore in logs ordered to be the ridge beams of

Wiley's Cozy Corner Sunset Rest Motel (local
residents only after previous identification)—

or as the bus driver between Victoria and Russell
(Kansas) ritualized at the end of the line:
"Last stop. Kindly let all those going out first."
(I have been free-associating past the assistant whom

and the blanks thereof. I might as well have been
inhaling Richard M. Nixon, the elephant's
capo dei capi, or some other maunder.) My son
is bored incommunicado. I am drafted to boredom

and must answer by name, rank, and serial number. It
ends. He, still sinus-smelling last night's pot,
goes off to his American-Dream-and-After
Seminar. I go for two eggs-up with bacon at Joe's,

garden for two hours, stir and reject the mail, and
doze off just in time for the 4:30 P.M. Great-Great-
Master-Marvel-Universal-Premiere (no Reruns ever)
Movie, which is all about carefully covered crotches.

When I wake to the trembling of the last, symbolized,
plagiarized, living-color veil, I find my son half
asleep in the other polar route chair to 9:00 inedible
o'clock A.M. "Well?" I say. "Hello, you old bastard,"

he says. So ends the trial of all assistant
whomnesses. Ours is no summary justice. We have
deliberated and found them guilty of being
exactly themselves. It does not, finally,

take much saying. There has even been time
to imagine we have said "Goddamn it, I love you,"
and to hear ourselves saying it, and to pause
to be terrified by *that* thought and its possibilities.

AND YOU?

I have met the queen who answers her bell naked.
She was interviewing an acid godhead for "Freak Out,"
writing his answers with seven felt pens in seven colors,
changing at random and often. It was a hot day.
In the ecstasy of his answers she kept hugging her pad
to wet breasts, staining them with transferred mess,
his answers lost in drippings from a light-show.

Where were you? Alan was here but left for the Ladies' Room
chanting Tibetan. A black gunner
shot down Dante in an anger beyond information.
There is no knowledge to make a man whole. There is—
I have seen it—ignorance that mislays him
till it multiplies into masses
and the daybreaking animal tide sets in.

Will you stay for the drowning? Students for a Drained Universe
will award posthumous flowers to the first 10,000
to dive with no questions asked. A guru who can float
will pass over the middle classes exterminating
Mother and Father with his conceptual shadow.
The police will be loved out of existence.
A manifesto named Bly will recite itself throughout.

Victrolas from City Lights will improvise
the lucidity of 20,000 Berkeley undergraduates
in a march toward radiance and sugar for all.
The combined casts of seven East Coast pornos
are sending immortal laundry, unwashed, from Jersey City
to Elko, Nevada, care of General Delivery.
If you have been given a name you may call for it there.

I have been thinking of Michelangelo's scaffolding
cross-stilting the Sistine Chapel like a happening,

then taken down with nothing left on the ceiling.
Is this like the grave of Kerouac? or only
a strewn lumber, like Timothy Leary's prose,
cluttering a psychic space equivalent to, maybe,
God, as mourned by Edward Dahlberg?

What's left when the man and the lumber come down
from the ceiling possibly good as God,
and nothing has happened? What allegory
is the corpse of the maker of nothing?
If some of the dust of Rome is from the hands
of a broken Buonarotti, then I have breathed
where bad air has been touched holy. And you?

AN EMERITUS ADDRESSES THE SCHOOL

No one can wish nothing.
Even that death wish sophomores
are nouveau-glib about
reaches for a change of notice.

"I'll have you know," it will say
thirty years later to its son,
"I was once widely recognized
for the quality of my death wish."

That was before three years
of navel-reading with a guru
who reluctantly concluded
some souls are bank tellers;

perhaps more than one would think
at the altitude of Intro. Psych.,
or turned on to a first raga,
or joining Polyglots Anonymous.

One trouble with this year's
avant-garde is that it has already
taken it fifty years to be behind
the avant-garde of the twenties

with the Crash yet to come.
And even free souls buy wives,
fall in love with automobiles,
and marry a mortgage.

At fifty, semisustained by bourbon,
you wonder what the kids see
in that Galactic Twang
they dance the Cosmic Konk to.

You will have forgotten such energy,
its illusion of violent freedoms.
You must suffer memory
to understanding in the blare

of a music that tires you.
There does come a death wish,
but you will be trapped by your
begetting, love what you have given,

be left waiting in a noise
for the word that must be whispered.
No one can wish nothing. You can
learn to wish for so little

a word might turn you
all the bent ways to love, its mercies
practiced, its one day at a time
begun and lived and slept on and begun.

GENERATION GAP

He parted a beard where his mouth might be—
an anatomical hypothetical—and said:
"Remember me, professor?"
                              "Smith," I told him,
"I forgot you the day you flunked
Freshman English for not meeting assignments
and you showed up for Soph Survey
where I forgot you with another F
and you showed up for Elizabethan Minors
and ditto and then for Remedial Illiteracy
which you did pass but with no reason
for keeping you anywhere in mind
except as so notably forgettable
that I made a note of it.
What are you doing in that shrubbery—
ambushing yourself?"
                        "How could I?"
he said. "I happen to know I'm here—
which rules out surprise, doesn't it?
I am a volunteer observer with instructions
to keep looking until someone asks
for my report."
                  "All right, Smith. Report."
"Thank God, sir! I was afraid it might all
be wasted."
              "What?"
                        "My endless observation."
"You have seen?"
                    "As through a glass darkly."
"Try removing your sunglasses."
"I did. It makes no difference
except that what's dark gets clearer
not brighter but deeper."
                            "You mean their eyes?"

"I mean behind them."
                          "Like looking
into a microscope?"
                          "How did you know?"
"And seeing your own eyelashes?"
"My own . . . ! My god, is that what I saw?"
"You realize, Smith, you have flunked again."
He shrugged. "My fate. I hadn't even known
I was taking the course."
                          "And mine," I told him.
"I hadn't known till now I was giving it."

ENCOUNTER

"We," said my young radical neighbor, smashing my window,
"speak the essential conscience of mankind."

"If it comes to no more than small breakage," I said, "speak away.
But tell me, isn't smashing some fun for its own sake."

"We will not be dismissed as frivolous," he said,
grabbing my crowbar and starting to climb to the roof.

"You are seriously taken," I said, raising my shotgun.
"Please weigh seriously how close the range is."

"Fascist!" he said, climbing down. "Or are you a liberal
trying to fake me with no shells in that thing?"

"I'm a lamb at windows, a lion on roofs," I told him.
"You'll more or less have to guess for yourself what's loaded

until you decide to call what may be a bluff.
Meanwhile, you are also my neighbor's son:

if you'll drop that crowbar and help me pick up this glass,
I could squeeze a ham-on-rye from my tax structure,

and coffee to wash it down while we sit and talk
about my need of windows and yours to smash them."

"Not with a lumpen-liberal pseudo-fascist!"
he sneered, and jumped the fence to his own yard.

There's that about essential consciences:
given young legs, they have no trouble at fences.

CITATION ON RETIREMENT

Light-Colonel Trinkett, you there
in the toe-crud of God's clay
feet, you ooze sliming the cellar
of data's orphan asylum, you loose
button of bloody threads numbering
haircuts to a follicle, you parade-rest
battalion of Wassermann positives
at close-order bedcheck zeroing in
demerit by demerit on a
recoilless maximum-velocity
fart in ranks; you light-stain,
belted-jelly leaking, ameoba,
virus, phagocyte, amino, ferment, down
porcelain filters to
chemistry's last edge of almost
life
  what's after you is back
to building blocks, space dust
in the galaxy of an alga's stoma
in the universe of a shrimp's rectum

Cross over, I say. Not drop dead—
that takes fallable substance—but
drain down one more
hole wrapped in a hole back to
exactly identified nothing

for the good of the service.

PARA DEREST

A meditation for 1967

Eyes right to Greek Revival
reviewing stands there on
the neo-grassroots Potomac,
the minutes of the meeting
tick to brass time. You
CAN hear eyeballs click
when Sarge volleys close-order
hellangone. He's the Q.E.D.
artillery's the logic of.

On, meanwhile, campus reading
one another's placards to
four letter WOW, I wait
lotused till my swami come.
Just one more drop now
of Godfloat acid and
I'll love you, do love you.

Can I find you? Addicts of
prime voids whorl skull walls.
Are you a color? Flower teeth
eat blue bits. In autumn
spectra fall. A vacuum-
cleaner cobalt cloud sucks me.

I'm freefall OM and won't
go bugling; oneliness
and refuse. It's rare here
falling in WOW. I crash
soft, bounce to orbit, and see
star slums rioting. Let's

picket a universe. This one
to start. UNFAIR TO APEMAN:
NO CONTRACT NO EVOLUTION.

My guru can't strike a
damn match for fear a
soul might burn (if
he knew how to rub its
head on his western pants) but
does know his Yankeedollar
take-home sutra.

              And Sarge,
he's dead—will be—
of untransubstantiating
slugs, the poor super-
establishmentarian meathead on
looting detail climbing figment's
memorized mountain of unfact.

Drop it, flower soul. Up OM.
There's no doing. There's
IS. There's UN-AINT. There's
easydrop tripkick. There's
swami payoff out of
squaredad's taxdodge. There's
cumshaw and untransliterated
acid and a shellhole smoking
in my head like God's wash-
bowl with the plug pulled,
the lava going down
clockwise   counterclockwise.
Goodbye, grime time. I'm
not going. I'm already
everywhere.

Don't you
go, man. Damn Sarge:
you squeeze his trigger
once, you get the recoil BOP
in the metempsychosis,
loose your connection,
drink unfluoridated
Ganges, get your placard ripped
where nobody likes it, and OOF
you're back in a louse, lover.

MEMO: PRELIMINARY DRAFT OF A
PRAYER TO GOD THE FATHER

Sir, it is raining tonight in Towson, Maryland.
It rained all the way from Atlanta, the road steaming
slicks and blindnesses, almost enough to slow for.
Thank you for the expensive car, its weight and sure tread
that make it reasonable to go reasonably fast.

My wife is in Missouri. She flew there yesterday
because her parents are eighty, terminal,
and no longer sure of what they were always sure of.
Thank you for airline tickets, rental cars,
the basic credit cards, a checking balance.

We doubt they can live much longer and not well.
I, too, have learned to love them. Thank you
for the wet roads to mercy on which I buy
the daughter home to the last of mother and father.
I wish I had such destinations left me.

I phoned my son at home tonight, the younger.
He has been busted for pot again. His fourth time.
There is, however, a lawyer, a reliable fixer.
He will cost me only another three days on this road.
Thank you for the road, the bad lunches, and the pleasant
    ladies.

I phoned my older son in Boston. He has wrecked his car
and has not learned to walk. His apartment, you see,
is almost a mile from school. He will miss classes.
Thank you for the classes he will not miss
if I ask my agent to book me a tour in April.

I phoned my daughter in New York. She is happy
but needs more voice lessons, and a piano.

She could make do with her guitar, but less well.
Thank you for everything she is dreaming of dreaming
and for the unanswered letter from California.

I will answer yes when I get home. The lessons
will come from pocket money. The piano
is waiting there in Claremont in February.
Thank you for Claremont and choices and for this daughter
and for the road I go well enough as things go.

I mean, sir, it does lead on, and I thank you.
It is not what I imagined. It may be better.
Better, certainly, than what I remember from starting.
At times, I confess, it is slightly depressing. The ladies
who are only slightly brittle and slightly silly,

but on any reasonable scale bright and admirable,
depress me slightly. But so do my own bad habits
when I am left to them freely. I do not complain:
I describe. I am grateful but imperfect and, therefore,
imperfectly grateful. It is all good enough

and I thank you, sir. If you are ever in Towson,
I can recommend the high level mediocrity
of the Quality Inn Motel just off the Beltway.
It is only slightly embalmed. It is clean and quiet.
With the TV on you do not hear the rain.